EMISSIONS MISSION!

By Brenda McHale

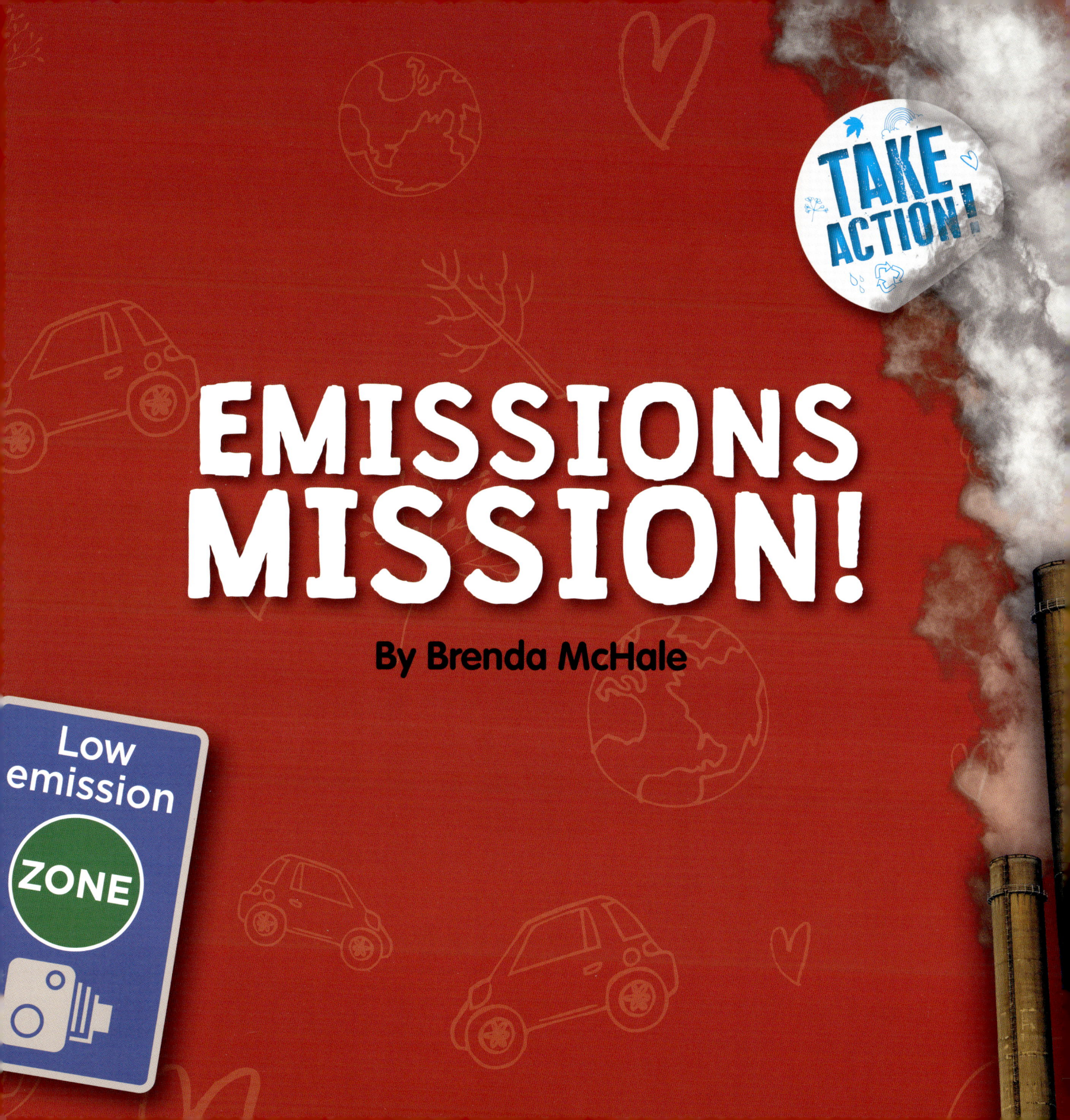

Low
emission

ZONE

BookLife
PUBLISHING

©2020
BookLife Publishing Ltd.
King's Lynn
Norfolk PE30 4LS

ISBN: 978-1-83927-107-6

Written by:
Brenda McHale

Edited by:
Madeline Tyler

Designed by:
Brandon Mattless

Words that look like **this** can be found in the glossary on page 24.

PHO

All image
Photo an
KUMAR, I
Peter Her
– aquatar
bibiphoto
Pagina, V
Pavel L Ph

ified. With thanks to Getty Images, Thinkstock
yGinzburg, Ody_Stocker, phil Holmes, JOGENDRA
nages – Kirill.Veretennikov, Katerina Davidenko,
-5 – Tartila, Triff, zorina_larisa Related keyw. 6–7
ir Melnik, volkova natalia. 8–9 – Africa Studio,
genbijl, John Williams RUS, PK Studio. 12–13 –
, Alexandre Rotenberg, Goldsithney, gorillaimages,
egam. 18–19 – Olena Yakobchuk, Baloncici. 20–21
– g215, Me..., business images, space-kraft, Yuganov Konstantin. 22–23 – Bloomicon, Sharomka, wavebreakmedia.

CONTENTS

Low emission

ZONE

NO PLAN(ET) B

Astronauts can visit space for a little time, but the only place that we humans can live all the time is on this planet, Earth. It's a great place to live.

Would you like to go into space one day?

Maybe one day, humans will live on another planet.
Until then, we should make it our mission to look after this one.

Animals and plants need us to look after the planet for them, too.

A BIG PROBLEM

Grown-ups haven't looked after Earth as well as they could have done. They've let it get into a bit of a mess.

Places are getting drier.

The sea is getting higher and damaging land.

Ice is melting and animals are losing their homes.

There are more forest fires.

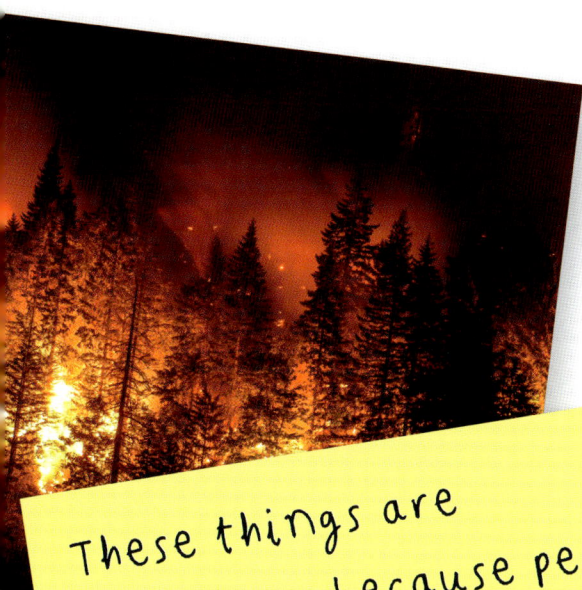

These things are happening because people have been doing things that are causing **climate change**. But it's not too late to stop this.

You might think this sounds a little bit scary. But don't worry – there are still lots of things we can do to help.

You might be thinking:

"What can I do about it?"

"I'm just a kid!"

Turns out, you can do a lot!

It's time to TAKE ACTION!

PROBLEM: EMISSIONS

Emissions are **gases**. They trap heat like a greenhouse and make Earth too warm. This is **harmful** for Earth and all the things living on it.

We need to cut emissions to stop climate change.

All these things **produce** emissions that are harming Earth.

Eating meat

Making electricity with gas and oil

Engine-powered **vehicles**

Buying lots of new things instead of fixing and reusing old things

RIDE YOUR BIKE!

Cars make lots of emissions. Cycling keeps the air healthier and helps you stay healthy, too. If you're going to visit a friend, ask if you can go on your bike instead of in the car.

Do you need a new bike? You could ask for a used one. Using things that someone else owned before stops new ones being made and that saves **energy**.

You may be able to find a used bike at a market or car boot sale.

TRAVEL TOGETHER!

For longer journeys, a train full of people doesn't produce as many emissions as a car for each person who is travelling. Trains can be faster and more fun too.

Buses have even lower emissions than trains. Buses that go a long way are called coaches.

If you have to travel by car, it's better if the car is full of people.

If there are lots of people travelling to the same place, maybe you could all go in one car.

13

STAY LOCAL

Travelling by plane is very bad for the **environment** because planes make lots of emissions. Instead of travelling by plane to go on holiday, lots of people stay in their own country and have fun.

By not going by plane, you might be able to take more toys on holiday!

What about not travelling at all? It could be fun to explore where you live. You might find exciting things to see and do just around the corner.

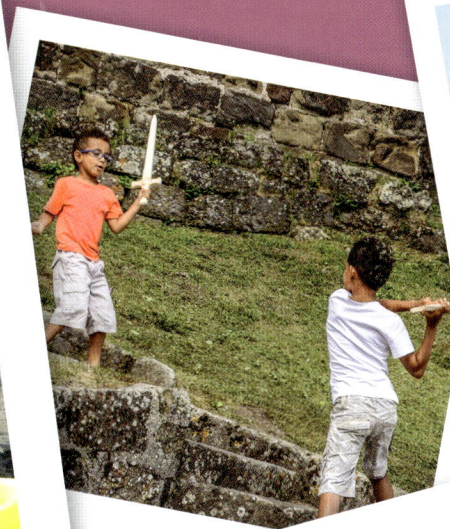

You can have a great holiday with no emissions!

MEAT-FREE MEALS

Farm animals that we use for meat produce harmful gas when they burp and pass wind. Can you think of some meals you like that don't have meat in them? You could ask your family to eat more meat-free meals.

Pasta and sauce without meat is just as delicious!

Lots of water and land is needed to keep animals for food. It takes a lot of energy to feed farm animals, too. Making all of this energy makes lots more emissions.

TAKE ACTION! Don't waste food.

TAKE CARE!

Power is needed to work all the machines that make things. Remember, using power means making emissions!

Machines like these make toys and other plastic things.

Most toys we buy are made in China. They travel from China in giant ships called container ships. The boats travel a long way and use lots of **fuel**. This creates lots of emissions.

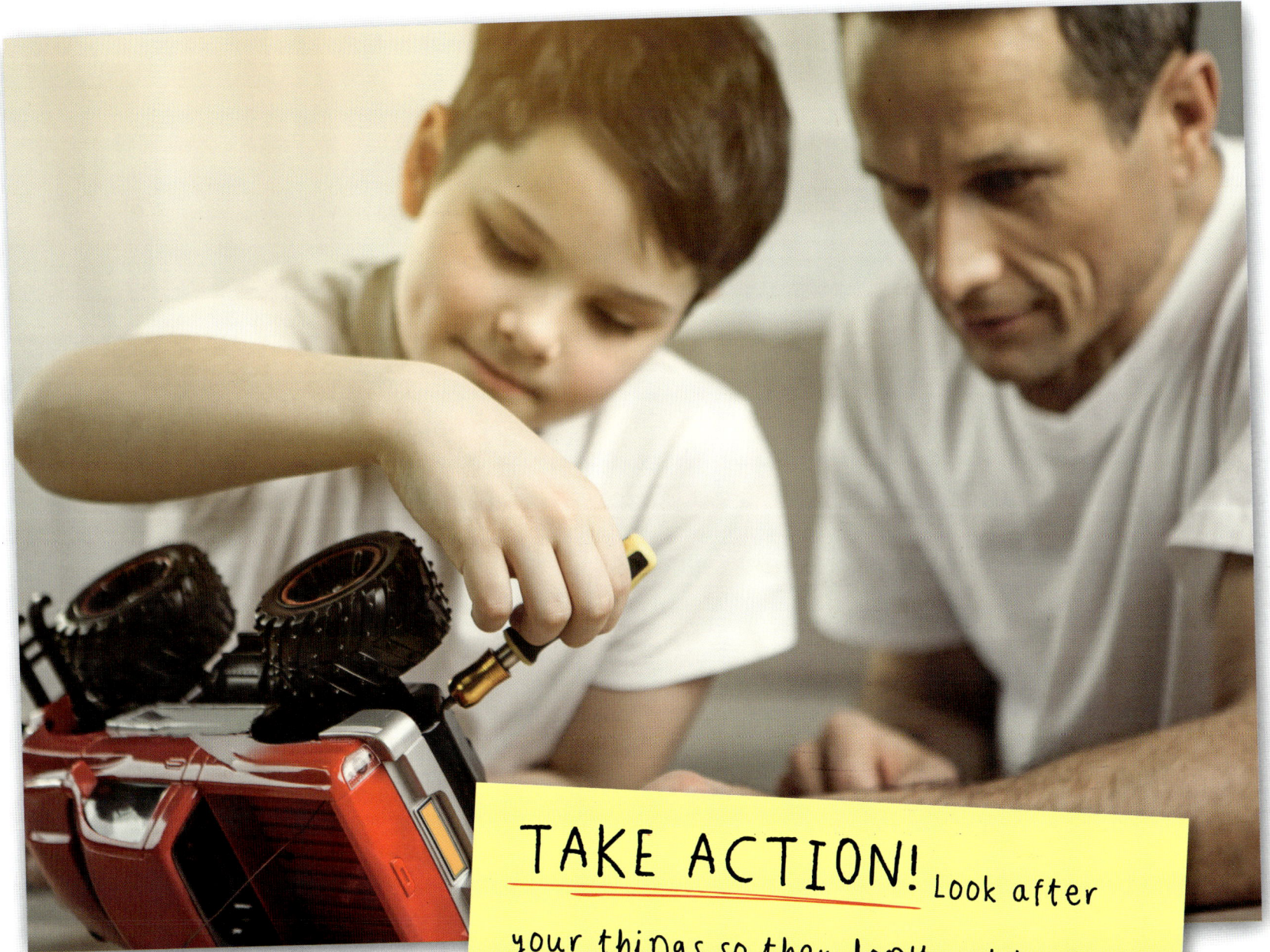

TAKE ACTION! Look after your things so they don't get broken.

GET IN THE KNOW!

There are other ways to cut your emissions. Remember, these actions cut your emissions because they save energy.

Having a shower uses less water and less energy than having a bath.

Don't throw things away if you can reuse them.

Switch off lights and the TV when you don't need them.

Making energy by using the Sun and wind is called renewable energy, or clean energy. The Sun and the wind will never run out, and they only produce a very small amount of emissions!

Have you ever seen a wind turbine like this up close? They're huge!

TAKE ACTION! Talk to your grown-ups about using renewable energy.

SPREAD THE WORD!

Isn't it exciting to learn about keeping the Earth safe? The best thing to do now is to spread the word. Tell your family and friends about the easy things they can do to help.

If your friends see you doing these good things, they might copy you. The more people who do these things, the easier the mission to save planet Earth will be!

GLOSSARY

climate change	a change in the temperature and usual weather of the world, which is harmful to all living things
energy	a type of power, such as light or heat, that can be used to do something
environment	the natural world
fuel	something that can be used to make energy or power something
gases	things that are like air, which fill any space available
harmful	dangerous or likely to cause harm
power	energy needed to make something work or do a job
produce	make
vehicles	machines that are used to carry people or things

INDEX